A CIRCUS OF WANT

THE DEVINS AWARD FOR POETRY

A Circus of Want is the 1992 winner of the Devins Award for Poetry, an annual award originally made possible by the generosity of Dr. and Mrs. A. Devins of Kansas City, Missouri. Dr. Devins was president of the Kansas City Jewish Community Center and a patron of the Center's American Poets Series. Since the death of Dr. Devins in 1974, his son, Dr. George Devins, has continued to sponsor the award.

A CIRCUS
OF WANT

Poems by
Kevin Stein

University of Missouri Press
Columbia and London

This book is for
Deb and Kirsten Anne.

Copyright © 1992 by Kevin Stein
University of Missouri Press, Columbia, Missouri 65201
Printed and bound in the United States of America
All rights reserved
5 4 3 2 1   96 95 94 93 92

Library of Congress Cataloging-in-Publication Data

Stein, Kevin, 1954–
    A circus of want : poems / by Kevin Stein.
        p.   cm.
    ISBN 0-8262-0843-6 (cloth : alk. paper).
    0-8262-0844-4 (paper : alk. paper)
    I. Title
    PS3569.T3714C5   1992
    811'.54—dc20   92-12350
                                          CIP

∞™ This paper meets the requirements of the
American National Standard for Permanence of Paper
for Printed Library Materials, Z39.48, 1984.

Designer: Kristie Lee
Typesetter: Connell-Zeko Type & Graphics
Printer and Binder: Thomson-Shore, Inc.
Typeface: Bookman Light

CONTENTS

♦♦♦

ACKNOWLEDGMENTS

Some of the poems in this book have appeared previously. Grateful acknowledgment is made to the following magazines: "The Music Time Makes," *Black Warrior Review;* "Gratitude," "How Things Fall," and "The Shrine," *Crazyhorse;* "It Didn't Begin with Horned Owls Hooting at Noon," *Denver Quarterly;* "In Absence and in Longing, Only Hunger," *5 AM;* "Out of Love, the Hideous Comes Unexpected" and "What I Meant to Say," *Indiana Review;* "Creatures Who Must Know Better Have Taken Me for a Blossom," *The Kenyon Review;* "The Virgin Birth," *The North American Review;* "Portraits" and "What I Know about the Eye," *Ploughshares;* "Birds in a Circle," "Terms," and "Whose Tracks Those Are," *Poetry;* "Angel" (under the title "A Circus of Want"), "In Love with a Middle-Aged Woman," "Rites for the End of a Drought," and "The WPA in Anderson, Indiana," *Poetry Northwest;* "A White Lie of Sorrow and Comfort," *Quarterly West;* "Anatomy Display," *Shenandoah;* "Before the Sirens There Was Red," *Spoon River Quarterly;* and "On the Ladder," *Southern Poetry Review.* In addition, some poems appeared originally in two chapbooks, *A Field of Wings* (Illinois Writers Inc., 1986) and *The Figure Our Bodies Make* (St. Louis Poetry Center, 1988).

I'm grateful for the generous support of the National Endowment for the Arts, the Illinois Arts Council, and the Peoria Area Arts and Sciences Council. Among those who offered advice and encouragement, special thanks is due James Ballowe, Dwight Brill, Ralph Burns, George Chambers, Roger Mitchell, Keith Ratzlaff, Maura Stanton, Dean Young, and mathematicians Michael McAsey and David Tudor.

♦♦♦

This world is all over dirty.

—Jonathan Edwards
from *Images or Shadows
of Divine Things*

I know what we call it
Most of the time.
But I have my own song for it,
And sometimes, even today,
I call it beauty.

—James Wright
from "Beautiful Ohio"

Angel

He carries it with him
everywhere, though "to carry"
implies two strong arms.
In fact he has none,
is bullet-shaped, really,
though he's not fired
from a cannon. He merely sits,
beneath a bright orange tent,
eating with his feet.

There is great dignity in this.
Grasping the utensils
between his toes, spooning
chicken soup, how he folds
the cloth napkin
when he's done. All this
for one token, a buck;
the fragrant elephants
cost two. I've watched
him in the library
at Peru, Indiana,
where the circus
sometimes winters,

his nimble toes
turning the pages of a book
on the ancient Sumerians,
who knew a thing
or two about disaster:
their homes flooded
or fields sere all summer,
those wandering, ignorant hordes

◆◆◆

who looted their cities
and smashed the cuneiform tablets
which told of Gilgamesh,

who, though he slew
many foes and earned great fame,
never got what he wanted,
either. I've watched a smile
crease his clean-shaven face,
and I've wondered about that,
his smile, I mean.
I mean, how does he not
hate us?

How do I, guilty
in my own body,
still ask for the muffler
to repair itself,
my apple tree to sprout
from its forlorn stump?
How can I not
wish to be an angel,
my left and right
given in solicitude?

1

Terms

This night we're drinking beer a pint
at a time, from Ball jars made in Muncie

where my wife and father were born. We're
doing this for no better reason, I think,

than to drink more and drink faster. Nostalgia
plays no part. The evening is coming on,

the low, wide prairie sky has begun to grey
in the fashion that sunsets take in here

when there's 90% humidity and no wind to urge
it elsewhere. No moon yet either, nothing

but the lazy twinkle of a star here and there
and the flashing red elegance of a light

atop the grain elevator. Somewhere beneath it
Varney sits on a three-legged stool with a flashlight

in his hands and a thermos of spiked coffee.
He's waiting for Linda to arrive, no doubt,

so they can move inside where the scales are read,
inside each other's baggy jeans and body, maybe

inside each other's soul. Each Tuesday before Linda
goes out, she wheels her husband to the bedroom,

turns on the television, and kisses him goodbye.
He's memorized this ceremony of the Purple Heart,

knows it as well as any Veterans' Day Parade
he's learned to sit through. Outside his window

and ours, too, a diaphanous fog has risen from the beans,
tempting us to name it good or bad, angel or serpent.

♦♦♦

Our black dog pauses in mid-field, surveying
the contour and design of the yellow flashes

that might be earth-bound stars, but are really just
fireflies blinking off and on. The males go high

and the females low while they signal their species
their need, their readiness. All this is true,

but I lied to you earlier. We're drinking
like this because we want a child and we can't

have one. "These things happen," the doctor said,
"These things you have to live with." Most nights

it's easy to feel inadequate, slightly broken,
thinking of the good or even the bad parent

you'll never have the chance to be. Honestly,
we're a little tiresome in our own despair,

which, after all, is not the despair of Varney
when Linda doesn't arrive, or Linda's that she's

not gotten her period, or anything like
that of her husband, who can't lie there

beside her without wanting to touch her
in a way that more than his mind can feel.

The Virgin Birth

Not that I ever believed it, or questioned it,
or really thought about what it
asked me to believe: how someone became
without becoming, how all at once He was,
of a sudden and the flutter of angel's wings,
without the touch of flesh to flesh,
without sweat, without pleasure or the swell
of pleasure that sweat confirms, without
the slightest matting of her unbraided hair
that day when nothing happened to happen
as if something had, as it did for me this morning,
when I whistled through chapped lips
and got nothing—not even the tiniest tune—

but still the dog came at a trot, each footfall
raising a child of dust which disappeared
into our galaxy, an ordinary spiral twirling
about a black hole among another 100 billion
some alien might call *nebulae* if she reads Latin,
or *home* if she's no fool. Why aren't I giddy
with the news every atom of iron in our blood
and calcium in our bones is the gift of a star?
Let me say I'm suspicious, let me say

I have my fears, even though my doubt
is not my father's doubt, bouncing his leg
to Basie's bass line at the Paramount Theatre
in 1939, when the knees of the girl he danced with
held the civilized world in place, sturdy
and predictable as the way she'd surely
clamp them shut. Four years later, hunkered down,
frozen to the frozen tundra of Attu,

he saw those legs kicking wild and open
as Andromeda apologized, invited him in
to the sky of perfect pleasure. It was hard

to believe in anything, let alone
that something could come of nothing,
a god made man to salvage him but not
his Japanese prisoners, their shaved heads
bowed and contemplative, here and there
a wound cherry-red and blooming
with what my father never called "star-stuff,"
though to one he handed his white handkerchief,
and got it back later, decorated,
Mt. Fuji sketched lightly in blood.

Birds in a Circle

I wouldn't argue, either, with the good fortune
of this: a circle of bare dirt, grass and seeds,
the warm jet of air the dryer spills out

to melt the snow. I've seen them perched
in the ash and black locust, among a familiar
stand of blackjack and bur and chinkapin.

Creatures of unreal design—a splotch of blue
or seasonal red, a yellow that's really more green.
They strike the pose of things with wings:

here now, gone now. But seeing them this close,
huddled in a circle of clear space, they look
too-perfectly made, ornaments hand-carved

and painted by my Vietnamese friends—Ly Bao
and Soo Kim, Matthew the son of Lu Ky.
Sometimes the things they make have fooled me:

birds red-bellied and black-capped,
the pileated and ruby-crowned static in mid-flight.
Come here, they say. *Touch me. I won't fly away.*

Still, kneeling in a window above these birds,
I don't move so they won't. This slant of morning,
particular and alluring, tempts me to believe

a thing so lovely it's absurd—that I could live here
forever, if only a wing weren't made for flight,
this body of mine so much dirt.

Gratitude

A gift, the boy's fall was.
Just as much as that pink duck
he carried around last Easter,
how it got weepy eyes and died.

Truth is, you can love too much,

and still his mother wraps him
in a blanket of arms while he sobs
and belches, his shoulder slightly wrenched,
young eyes startled open.

So this is how it feels,
those eyes say, *to be grounded.*
To have your sudden rise
come to a perpendicular stop
beneath the maple.

I've come to do the neighborly thing,

though the only words I find to say
sound like the breath shoved from his lungs,
the gasp that isn't a gasp at all
but an awful suck for air to billow-out
the flat, deflated bags in your chest.

I don't want to lie,

I should tell him about my own fall
from the backyard ailanthus,
the way its stink became more beautiful
as I dropped—reaching,
bringing down a few leaves with me.

My mother, busy with the dishes,

♦♦♦

didn't see or hear a thing
when I fell in the bare spot
where the batter's box was.
Dust rose like the cloud of breath
lifted from me: my visible soul

a mortal persuasion.

Out of Love,
the Hideous Comes Unexpected

though I'm not thinking of the lovers' bed
but the plants beside it—flattened,
bent, some broken, all of them burdened
by pillow or blanket, your shoe
so hard to kick off. And not
the day lily itself, but what
its name implies, the orange
and yellow bloom of consequence.
Not even the September frost,
or our worry, but sheets embossed
with mud, windblown and strung
along the fence, flapping as if
the whole yard were sailing back
to blue-stem prairie.

                         Some mornings
before coffee, before the bathroom
has lost its bone-white gloss,
its chill and antiseptic fury,
some mornings every act implicates another,
as a moment ago, braving a look
in the mirror, my eyes blurred
and seemed to cross the way
my mother threatened they would
if I didn't cut it out. I saw
her thin and serious face, the upswept
hair, her curious butterfly frames
rising from her eyes like baroque angels,
I swear it.

◆◆◆

It's not the angels
that worry me as I open the blinds,
but the quick yank and thwack of wood
on wood like a fist greeting your teeth,
a feeling I remember from that evening
fixing dinner at a girlfriend's house
while her parents slept it off,
that evening she asked me to pray
the rosary for her father's cure,
her mother's black eye, but most
for the meter-reading job
and her moving out. We knelt
in the kitchen, bacon spitting
grease on us, white toast
hardening to bird food. Then we
knelt in her room.

What I remember
is she caught hell when they walked in
on us, I got thrown out, and her father
started drinking with a vengeance so acetylenic
his Ford nearly severed the light pole
at Fifth and Lincoln, the whole block
gone black. What we do we do out of love,
ignorance, loss—their endless permutations
strung like beads on a chain. Who can say
how far it stretches or if it will return—
disguised as the handsome stranger,
perfect as lightning to a blasted tree.

In Absence and in Longing, Only Hunger

(Goiania, Brazil, 1987)

The sign for the word, which is itself
a sign, meant nothing to them.
Only yellow and black, bad art.
The men had split the lead canister
with an eight-pound sledge,
earning their day's junkyard pay.
As night was falling, the radioactive cesium
glowed more beautifully than normal,
and women came from all around to rub it on
their faces and dance while the men sang.
The face of each took on a ghostly,
aquamarine hue, more passionate than oceanic.
One, so moved, dabbed it on her pert nipples, giggling
as they glowed beneath her cotton blouse.
But Leide Ferreira, age 6, knew this
was the second coming of the Christ.
She put some in her pocket for safekeeping,
and with thumb and index finger, delicately placed
a wafer in her mouth as if it were a host
brighter than all of Father Santiago's,
then slowly crossed herself and swallowed.

The Music Time Makes

(With a line borrowed from Plutarch)

The neon big apple had begun its slow
serenade of a fall, and so many voices
spilled from televised Times Square
that none could be heard, only
a raucous and unrelenting din
that, if carefully listened to,
sounded like the heart thumping
in a lover's chest. Meaning
noise is a relative disaster,
meaning we distrust beauty
the way autumn trees in San Francisco
still shed their leaves, disbelieving.
Guy Lombardo, who's gone, was not playing
"Auld Lang Syne" when a friend extended
his hand, and without a note of humor
or vanity said, "I love my life."
I've loved mine as the wasp
trapped between panes loves his—
calmed by the sun's aria,
delighted by its promise of escape.
Think of the good luck of some.
Say, Alcibiades, beautiful traitor,
who, given the friendship of Socrates
and all manner of loveliness, betrayed it—
yet *"bloomed all the ages of his life."*
Cuffing strangers for fun, boxing the ears
of teachers who wouldn't teach Homer,
Alcibiades rose lazily and more lovely
from the ashes of his destructions,
as did my brother-in-law, who once put
Pat Metheny's "Still Life (Talking)"

♦♦♦

into his son's tape player, mistakenly
pushed *record* along with *play*
and went about his work. Fifteen minutes
passed before he missed the music
and played back what he'd recorded,
his worksong: the *thump thump thump*
of footsteps on newly built stairs,
nails being sunk, his *damn*
for a hammered thumb.

What I Meant to Say

If a sentence is a journey perilous
with distraction, and each word
a forest to get lost in, an enigma
of slash-marked trees and little
plastic ribbons, the whole of it
desperate with beauty that flits
and wings about as Plato's birds did—

if this is true, then beware
of the spaces between words,
those clearings doused with light
and spackled with sweet william,
cornflower, coreopsis, a place
ablaze with blue flax where you
might sample an apple or pear,
then turning to go turn east
instead of west, head back
where you've been, not where you've not.

Whoever's the keeper of truth,
tender of the walled garden
or whatever myth we can agree
to disagree on, whoever that is
is stingy, querulous, probably mad.
Why else so little of it, why else
my ignorance passing for good intentions

when she got home from work,
soul corroded and nearly yellowed
from her day of leaching kidneys;
when she got home, wanting nothing more
than to take her shoes off,
why else should I ask, "Why don't

♦♦♦

you cut your hair?"— meaning,
"It's lovely worn short."
Meaning that now I mean to say,
"Forgive me,"

though nothing's that simple.
If words are merely signs,
what then are these: the dog's whimper,
a child's cough behind closed doors,
any woman's cry when she blesses love,
a note tensile and pulsing
that leads to the inevitable pause,
pause when nothing, not even breath,
moves? And this silence, too,
says *soon, soon* as surely
as a plowed field does.

Whose Tracks Those Are

Again the February hearts strung about
in shapes that defy physiology: the red
too red, curves too curved, the slotted
absence too full of white to show what
absence really is. This is the morning

of no defense. You've opened the parakeet's
cage and let her fly around, crapping
where she wants. This is the day
the dog gets a bath, her fleas poisoned
and washed away, your beige carpet cleaned.

This is a morning for biding time,
newspaper filler read column by column
as you line the cage. How, for instance,
one family has tended its sacred fire
for 1,128 years—a period into which

you must factor murder, pestilence, and
infertility; in which you must take account of
crop failure, war, and laziness. Think of
the morning you had a cough and the air
was chill at the temple, or when you drank

too much the night before and God Herself
drummed Her seven hands upon your head,
or imagine a day like this one, awaiting
test results, when finally a voice
like moonlight cradling snow tells us

the baby inside my wife has died.
This is the day the plants need watering.
We'll do it stiff-legged, automatic—
the earth reeling beneath us as it must
beneath the fainting goats we read about,

those fearful ones who grow rigid and collapse
upon hearing any distant shriek. But this
is a morning to keep the flame. Lay down
the lance and shield, put off our armor.
Unsaddle the tawny horse, let him find his way.

2

♦♦♦

Anatomy Display

Woman and Horse
Illinois State Museum,
Springfield, Illinois

Whoever sold them as a package,
endlessly haggling over their price,
whoever mounted them beneath a universe
of glass, must by now be like them

(empty-eyed, all bone), though not
deployed as she is, forever in mid-stride,
held by a metal pole rising cold
from the floor through her pelvis,

climbing her spine like fear,
capped by thick cork and her skull set
slightly askance the horse, who rears
as if he knows us for what we are.

Once, in Kashmir, she tended the temple flame,
a keeper of Vishnu, the god who watched
her every step toward death, which came
with sudden rain upon his candles,

that hissing last breath, her body
not worthy of burning but left
to rot until an Englishman saw profit
in calling her a princess, a lie

which got her bones to Chicago
before the money gave out. There,
she wed the Belgian workhorse,
thick-shouldered, stout, who'd collapsed

♦♦♦

at the plow and was sold in disgust.
If work is the essence of Being,
some dismal account of what it is
to be you or me, if work is what

we leave behind more than spouse
or child or deeply mortgaged house,
if work is what we are and were,
then many of us fail, as did these two,

distracted by a clear bowl of sky
or thunder rumbling in clouds,
the heart thump-thumping in our chest;
many of us will go to our rest

with gutters still leaking, that treatise
on Schiller unwritten, with a box
of understanding still unopened
in the corner. And though I'm not

about to agree that we're only
what we do, for surely we're as much
what we refuse, it's true that most
won't earn a second chance, as did

the woman from Kashmir, to show us
what human really is. Bound in time
to a horse she never fed or curried
or brushed, coupled by bright wires

of our ignorance—her mandible to his,
femur to femur, carpals to that hard place
above the hoof, her body insisting,
"This is us, this is not."

How Things Fall

There's the intuition of a key
about to enter a lock, familiar
and confident as a foot poised above
a worn sock. That's not what

made him leave their darkened house
in favor of the yard, its cool
September breeze. It wasn't a notion
of anything he could say out loud,

or even how hard she'd slapped him,
that made him look to the bathroom,
its lush, golden GE light
spilling out the open window.

What turned his head was the thunk
of acorns dropping through the huge
bur oak, what startled him with a picture
as clear as Newton's of how things fall.

His wife, seated on the tub, was masturbating
with left and right hands—head arched,
neck and shoulders flushed, both eyes
closed. Drawn to her now the way the man

at the liquor store is drawn to pain,
the guy who punches his own face for quarters
to buy Mad Dog 20/20, he crouches
at the threshold and listens as she groans,

Fuck me, oh fuck me, Davey, a name he'd never
heard her say in such anger or bliss,
in sickness or in health. And since
it is not his name, given or otherwise,

and since he cannot bear her name
for infidelity, or his own list—Windy
(with an "i"), Cindy, Stacy, Heather—
he crawls on his belly through the wet,

welcoming fall ground to the osage-orange
and their puke-green hedgeapples,
nearly fluorescent in the harvest moon.
They look like brains to him, as human

and useless against the body's yearnings
as his own. He smashes a few against
the hard trunks of hedge trees, eats
the spongy center and prays that

his mother, who only meant to warn him,
was right about their poisons.
And all he can think to do is ask God,
Please don't let me vomit.

On the Ladder

It's the gravity
you notice,
the unceasing urge
of things to drop,
as if their spiraling
descent were a kind

of ascension, a fruition.
Never mind the results—
your brush speckled with dirt,
the roller having stained
an incline it shouldn't have,
you on your butt in pain—

falling is a state of grace.
A friend of mine, who's never
painted a lick, contends
being on a ladder is a
metaphysical experience, something
about Kant and the nearness

to God. I don't know.
My arches ache, knees burn,
my hamstrings taut as clothesline,
but I'm not ready to come down
even a rung or two, when
I hear the thunder and feel

the first few drops that marshal
my descent from the borrowed ladder
my father cried on back in 1972,
when it began to rain, and he heard
that my pale uncle, muscles gone
to jello, had fallen face up.

♦♦♦

Voices

Were it only the toaster that spoke to them,
they might've coped, learned to live with WBZZ radio
invading their privacy at inopportune moments.
Take the time they lay in bed, just beginning,
and the bedroom radiator bellowed the voice
of Jim Morrison, urging "Come on, come on now,
touch me babe." That was OK. But Neil Meyers,
the talk-net pseudo-shrink, dispensed advice
from their oven, and golden oldies railed all night
on the pipes to the used Maytag. What's more,
a Baptist preacher's Sunday morning broadcast
interrupted her mother's weekly phone calls,
proclaiming the Lord's Providence in all things earthly
and divine, which both of them took as a sign.
    They moved.

The thing is, when home alone, they felt alone
without the voices. They wondered what happened
to the man whose wife cheated on him while he was gone
to Broker's classes. Their own lives seemed small,
withered by happiness to a set of two,
where two meant null set, meaning empty.
They'd listened so long they'd forgotten how to talk.
One day while his wife was out for a run,
he called Dr. Joy Brown, whose voice he liked a lot.
He told her everything: about the toaster,
the radiator and Jim Morrison, about a dream he'd had
that language was sexual only when disembodied,
electromagnetically reproduced and sent travelling
on its own to be heard, and judged nakedly,
by total strangers. Dr. Brown urged him
to share this with his wife, which he was going to do.
But she'd heard it all on her portable radio ear phones,
and there was no need to say a word.

◆◆◆

Before the Sirens There Was Red

sky with greenish tint,
wind heavy with contempt
for oak, ash, the last-ditch elm,
a train approaching when none was due.

All the signs, and the signs said,
Dorothy and Toto, bye bye.

In the town we call a village,
street lights sizzled, popped,
and glass blew in the eyes of the girl
pumping gas at Ducky's, her face

becoming a blossom, some lovely

unlovely which shaped the bluster
as a body sculpts empty space.

But this is only counting backwards,

a progression of mind which naturally ends
with me on Carlene's porch, the wind
fierce and drunken like the father
who wanted her so badly,

so badly he wanted her he swung
the glass door shut on her raised hand,

which doctors sewed together to resemble a hand,
and it never grew. The little hand
she used to touch boys with in high school,
to make them seem happy, and it big.

The WPA in Anderson, Indiana

The elephant had just had enough.
Too many small towns without rivers,
too many tents to raise, the pasha
gone forever. So when he sat down there
on the hood of a Chevy, no one stared.
They had not cared for the ease of his
forgetting a job he was called to do.
Not there in front of Al's Cigars,
the line of unemployed trailing off
to dirty sidewalk.

Now Ginny Marie fusses, and behind us
a row of pocket tee-shirts understands
why she cries. We've filed past
the Peek 'N Booze so many times
no one bothers to look inside. The dancers
make familiar moves, like wives or daughters.
Today is August enough for us, and this one
redbird sings in a tired ailanthus,
its bark split and smelling of stinkwood,
and still he sings.

In Fatima the Virgin appeared, asking
for rosaries. Instead our fathers
worked the WPA, and bent at their waists
they turned the face of this street.
When exhaust rises from cars, we see them
carrying hod. We remember Fifth Street
right side up, the worksong of bricks
turned top for bottom.

The Shrine

My mother wants to visit the latest shrine
to Jesus. Not the face rusting on a settling-tank
out East, but His face on a dying man's
bathroom window somewhere in California.
Her neighbors are going, making the four-day drive
from Indiana with their son who stutters,
hoping to cure the boy and my mother.
Strange, but she's worried about me.
I've been reading about Germany, the fatherland.
I'm thinking of going there to visit
the chalk artists in Trier
who sketch on the cement sidewalk.
"A shrine to impermanence," the catalog says,
"human transience enacted in chalk."
High above the forgiving Rhine,
two brothers who couldn't get along
built dueling castles and murdered each other's serfs.
At night they'd signal to each other,
"I hate you," and in the morning,
torches burning, "I still hate you."
I have no enemy to signal, no one to bring
his blessed face so near I can punch it.
When this disease finishes with her,
she'll look something like them: the whites
that billow-out against a blue sky hurrying to grey,
shorts and tee-shirts that fill with air,
rise full-blown, then drop.
Call in the dog, it's going to rain.

Some Lunar Effects
(for D. L. S.)

Though the moon pours its liquid self
through the slats of the half-closed blind,

it does so precisely and with an artist's
attention to detail. *Look at me*, it insists,

giving its best impersonation
of sunlight come home late and drunk,

a little randy. This is the full moon
of pull and sway and swagger—

its nightly habit of rise and rise
and languid descent tonight so suddenly

articulate even the dishwater
in the sink seemed tidal as it rose

about my wrists. It wasn't hard then
to imagine the apprehensive mood of Rod

at Rod's Pour House. How he might hurry
to tap a fresh keg of Bud, keeping his eye

on patrons who wait impatiently, hands plunged
in their bulging pockets. It wasn't hard, either,

to think of the babies who'll surge this night
from their mother's small seas and scream

at their headfirst dive. While I'm at it,
I'll admit the ease of letting go,

giving way. And I think it's only fair
to warn you that I am moved, too,

♦♦♦

that you might awaken to my face looming
above yours in our bed—my face round

and familiar as that one in the sky.
Or better yet, let me be warned on such a night

that any minute now you might turn off
this late-inning game, drain my half-mug

of beer and aim it for the couch.
Not even bother with the light.

Come up, you'd say, *I have something for you.*

Natural Law

1

In a room above us, the first few thumps
of pleasure, the headboard beating a quick heartbeat
against the wall. And the muffled, tight-throated

cry of giving way, her voice unfamiliar, raspy;
then his, suddenly a bright ruby encircling
her neck, now hard, as if no value lay

in letting go what had been long coming.
Willingly, we turn in bed and kiss—under
no obligation to uphold the doubledater's oath

that says front and back seat couples must go down
together and rise back up simultaneously:
perfectly disheveled, imperfectly reborn.

No, we kiss for us, for the dog who's just discovered
the killdeer's nest set down in low stubble,
for the female who wails from the uncut timothy,

and the male who must look as ridiculous
as he is futile—prancing, bobbing,
even feigning a broken wing that begs

Come get me. This is the state of things
at our home, circa 1987, no different from
the revelation of 1629 when Galileo's telescope

showed all matter is a passing fancy: an idea
which earned him tenure, a promotion, and papal censure.
Still, that must've amazed him less than this universe

of fractured symmetry, where a broken whole
gives depth to its unbroken parts. Take, for instance,
the girl in the morning paper, who fell 17 stories,

split a silver maple, then fell two more—and lived.
On the editorial page a scholar proves

♦♦♦

she'd not reached her terminal velocity of 79 mph,

that she was saved by a maple sapling
and the laws of a universe describable by
differential equations: $y'' - 1.8y' = -g$.

2

At breakfast, red on red, the color of lips
pressed on lips, that's the shade our mouths take.
Deliberate and unashamed, these friends

(she's 40 and desperate for a child,
he's 31 but unlucky), they gladly spread
their toast with cranapple jam and listen

as my wife begins our story, a perverse litany
of fertility tests and tubals, histosalpinograms
and clomid prescriptions, her D+C and my ejaculating

in a plastic cup. How each morning's temperature,
each time and place and position was charted
and graphed, rated for efficiency. Now she pulls

the last-month's record from the drawer, explains
the circles and dots. Proving Aristotle's theory
that two forces govern all the universe,

she lifts from her chair and sits back down,
rises and descends with each basal temperature
she's pointing to. She stops on a red dot,

"That's it, July 13th, my parents gone out
for supper, there in my girlhood bed,
a child." There's crazy music in her voice,

a half-loony tune in time with the awful wailing,
in motion with the girl's pitiful fall, in keeping
with the notion—half crazy itself—that our joy

might last, starched and rising like a pink crinoline,
that it might hold the weight of our friends' despair
as this skirt of stars presses down.

◆◆◆

Creatures Who Must Know Better
Have Taken Me for a Blossom

This year Kennebec and Red Pontiac,
last year's russet and white kobblers
done in by nematodes, flea beetles,
early and late blight. Maybe it's
the ¼ Irish blood that's made me drunk
with promise, though wasn't it Ali,
stung by his loss to Holmes,
who explained it, "I had the world,
and let me tell you, it wasn't nothing"?
You see, I cut them as if they were diamonds,
with a studied, precise stroke. *All this,*
the voice of reason reminds me,
for what I could buy in a reusable
mesh bag. But I'm stubborn
in the middle of God's own metaphor
dropping potatoes into loamy dirt,
while ruby-throated hummingbirds
take my red shirt for the biggest bee balm
they've ever seen. Their wings flapping
at an angel's pace, they taste my only
holiness, my sweat. I want to tell
my father what's happened, tell him
I'm sorry, I didn't mean to drink too much
and sleep it off on the job he got me,
didn't mean to get caught by a man named Earl
who had no eyebrows and was his boss.
None of that was planned any more
than he'd planned on the family's
Salvation Army clothes, his cars that never ran,
those late-night trips upstairs to bleed

◆◆◆

the radiators, or turn off a fan,
any reason to stand a while
and watch us sleep. After Mass
the children would go to grandmother's garden
to weed, water, and sometimes dig dinner
in our underwear, while she washed
our Sunday suits and we kids pretended
to be flowers.

It Didn't Begin with Horned Owls
Hooting at Noon

Though in them he heard   the weird symmetry
of loss and love's becoming,   a great silence
between one call and the   other's reply.
So he laid block, framed   studs into walls:
plumb, square, on line.   He stayed up late,
straightening bent nails   on the lip of a block
with his ballpeen hammer,   the way a contractor
with a sprung back had shown   him. Evenings
he went next door to talk,   toting his thermos
of bitter coffee and a picture   of his son
who's dying of AIDS. Son   he'd failed, son
he'd pounded on and never got   right. When he
was ready to hang sheet rock,   he penciled on
women with bulbous breasts   and legs
he'd spread wide, women bent   at the waist
as if in supplication to   some irremediable need
only his hand could quiet.   Then he hung
the rock with his women   facing him, sometimes
sawing them in two.   On the morning he finished
he rolled paint over   each and all of them.
Every wall white   in the room where his son,
forgiving him,   was coming home to wait.

◆◆◆

Portraits

It's not the chapel bell at Arles,
only a door bell rung on television,
but it's enough to send the dog
in a scurry and yapping to the front door
where no one is. I'm not Gauguin,
at least not now, the isle of Tahiti
has disappeared into the ether of possibility,
and the girls, too. All a dream.
What's there to say but yes,
these are my legs and doughy middle,
this is my face beginning to wrinkle,
these hands mine, blunt-fingered, small.
Yes, it's only the house I've been painting
on long summer days, and no, nothing's exotic
about my dreaming of the islands,
a place I longed for but never got to
in my unbridled youth. Maybe it's
the heat, or maybe the paint,
but I imagined us sitting in the almost
fluorescent ocean, under a great inverted bowl
of blue sky, drinking beer in the afternoon.
This, for chrissake, this could've happened
as easily as it didn't for me and Dana,
who, wounded at Da Nang, came home
to kiss my sister on our front porch
as if it were nothing. He gave her
a black-velvet Elvis. A forlorn,
sort of disembodied Elvis
whose brown eyes looked as evanescent
as the voice of reason in 1969.
Then he went back, and didn't
come back. This morning's heat so rose
like a blister from the shingles, and waves

♦♦♦

so shimmered above a green sea of beans
that the beauty of dog in shade,
child in red wagon, and wife in garden
offered an angle of declamation I'd seen
once in Gauguin's "Riders on the Beach."
Four riders depart under a turbulent sky,
while pale riders on still-paler horses
intersect their path unseen. Gauguin
thought of the pale ones as spirits, as life
playing out its endless what-might've-beens,
as even now I stand at the burst-open screen door
and call, *Come home boy, come home,*
unable to see or hear what's out there,
what's not.

What I Know about the Eye

After our daughter's last milk
and fruit, long after the bath's
tugboat and its cargo of plastic squares
and yellow ducks has docked on the tub,
after her tooth-brushing that amounts to
nothing more than sucking the paste
from the brush, she begins another ritual
of *afters* meant to postpone her going down
for good: a hug for the bear wearing
my Little League cap from Glassmakers Local 777;
then to Mickey in the corner and Donald
beside him, Pinocchio whose nose
has darkened from the press of small hands;
finally to the barred-zoo of her bed
and night-night pats for Bugs
and Raggedy Anne. After her night
light's in, the shade drawn down tight,
after the good night kiss we give
and she gives with a wet smack
of her lips, we ascend to quiet so alarming
it frightens us outside where crickets
start and restart their small engines,
where fog drifts from the cut of a creek
that drops through Kickapoo to the Illinois
and Mississippi rivers, and from there
God knows where in the casual embrace
of the sea. I'll admit to hugging
the bear myself, while homeless families
sleep on sidewalk grates and children
go hungry in every latitude and longitude
of this world that Berkeley swears
our minds make in the image we wish of it,
our seeing both creation and illusion.

◆◆◆

When I close my eyes, the destitute face
of the Other lingers there, inside,
a black reproach to my careful happiness.
Yet when I open them again, the moon glows
above me like the luminescent Jesus
poised on the dash of my parents' Chevy—
arms spread wide, his heart open
and rising like mine.

In Love with a Middle-Aged Woman

You could say it wasn't much—
the lone sprig of iris
leaning in a chipped vase off-centered
on the table,

among the unread newspapers
and (forgive me)
last night's dishes.

You might contend two of its blooms had wilted,
or that choosing white was itself
refusal,
an innocence.

You might even dismiss the gesture
as just that,
meaningless
as a cloud's undressing
grey to purple to white again,
no rain.

You would be right,
partially and of ill humor,
until you sit a while
and enter
the unfolding center
where scent resides,

witness petals close around you
like the blossom it is.
And water,

always water,
though not exact cascades
but a glistening
in the petals

◆◆◆

that falls like beads fall
from your breasts.

On the table
arcs of sullen pollen,
continents of desire shifted
by each stray breeze,

worlds made and unmade
as surely as gravity
beckons a petal-drop,
the bloom of you,
that perfect undoing.

The Physics of Free Will

Last night the saleswoman showed me how the graphics
of a computer produce mere orthogonal projections.
She drew shapes I remembered from physics
and geometry, from Mr. Chezem who had a flat-top.
Then smiling at me she paused and said,
"It's like the etch-a-sketch you played with as a boy,
or that sailor with a beard of iron filings."
I had no use for the deluxe model, but I bought it,
I'm afraid, because the woman was good looking,
or because she compared it to nostalgic items,
or worse, because she wore powder blue.

Things happen the way they do, I'm thinking now,
because they're supposed to. I don't believe that,
but I doubt if it's free will that urges the two
barred owls—one low and one high-pitched voice—
to ask questions of first cause, of identity,
absence. Before morning they call out, moving
like points on a grid, each a function of the other.
If their voices were beams of light
they would sketch a parabola of sound made visible
to the angels, who can't even hear the drone
of the heart, a most simple pump.

Things happen the way they do because
they have to. It's simple, I tell myself,
thinking of the fly that followed an over-ripe
cantaloupe inside the refrigerator, determined
for one last taste. Tonight under this bright scimitar
of moon, it's easy to remember the vision of hell
a priest told me in the confessional: to be made
forever to watch reruns of your life's worst decisions,

to speak in penance, "Coaches, lovers, friends,
I couldn't help myself." But if there's no free will,
then there's less hell for us in hell
than on earth, where each effect will find its cause
like iron drawn to a pole it can't refuse.

Contingencies

The little twinge she feels
at seeing our infant daughter bleed
is not little at all.
Having snipped Kirsten's finger
along with the nail,
my wife cries—not like a baby—
but with passion to match
this declaration of what's to come.
All morning we'd circled the garden
with chicken wire,
and yesterday adorned
the cherry tree with a net
to shut the bluejays out.
Innocent, foolish, plain stupid.
None of this matters now
that our daughter's finger bleeds
and jays, the usual bullies,
writhe broken-winged in that net.
Our labrador scurries, her eyes
implying that she saw it coming,
what with all the trouble
we'd had clipping her big dog nails.
The precise tone of her whining,
blending with those birds' awful racket,
the child's tearful wailing,
a wife's sobbing, and this screaming
I excuse as my own excited voice,
registers a familiar B minor,
then a crescendo of what must be
cymbals and timpani drums,
and I recall with trepidation
the warning printed on a compact disc
version of the 1812 Overture:

♦♦♦

DANGER: DIGITAL CANNONS.
And though there's no explosion,
I'm not a father who knows best,
and she's not my gaunt-faced
little Princess. There's just
a life, this life we open
like a borrowed manila envelope,
into which we put ourselves,
our souls, oh everything
the milky sky might rain on us
and cause to grow as red
as the blood-red peonies
my mother calls *pi-ah-nees,*
a discernible pining in the way
she says it, in the way she takes them,
ants and all, to my Uncle Sandy
who's so limp from muscular dystrophy
that he can't move his hand,
or even his little finger,
to wave bye-bye.

◆◆◆

Rites for the End of a Drought

I had not thought to wait so long.
I'd almost forgotten its tune,
the plink, plink, plunk of it
in the eaves, its rhythm and
surprise, how the sky's blue
then grey, the way it happens
to happen. For once this summer
no sun threatened our black dog
with instant heat stroke. She
sat in the dead grass and waited,
anticipation so green in her brown eyes
I sat with her, and when it came,
rain, I rolled in the wet grass, too,
first shirtless, then shortless,
then naked as the dog, wild as the boy
who slept on the porch the night
a circus paraded through town,
his balls aching, anticipating
the sequined women whose bodies
gleamed in low-cut splendor,
their spike heels sexual
on the hard brick. I remember
how a tinny band echoed
through the corridor of frame houses—
white and beige and white
all red in a flash of the sheriff's
cherry-top. Parents watched
from the windows, but kids
were on the curb when the elephant
sat his ass down on the hood
of John Stolley's Chevy.
We cheered the drunken clowns,
glared at the bearded lady,

♦♦♦

worried for the world's
fattest boy, 12 years old
and already 527 lbs. When
it was over, everyone gone back
to bed, bricks wet and shining
under the street light, I found
a box turtle on its back,
some circus man's prize
spilled from a wagon of chance.
To be honest, I took him to keep him,
but in the morning, ripe with guilt,
I headed for the Fair grounds.
The thing is, you see, I rested
in the shade of the Singing Bridge,
and prayed for divine guidance, which came
in the form of sleep, so subtle but clear,
so deep his brindle shell was not there
when I awoke in rain.

A White Lie of Sorrow and Comfort

My daughter's right,
though something's always lost in the telling,
even the glint of surprise
when she told her mother,
"I hugged a bird today."
It goes like this:
the world she hoped for
simply *is*—
the snowfall only a blanket,
those doves merely sleeping
when she presses a frozen bird
against her chest,
that sky a tumble-down grey
and she never guessing.

I've heard what you don't know
can't hurt you,
how a blessed ignorance seals friendships
and preserves marriages,
that happiness can be so beautiful on the branch
you shouldn't pick it,
but I should tell her the one
about her father in a late autumn orchard,
when the last McIntosh hung round and perfect,

so lovely I reached from below
expecting fullness,
but got instead a shell nearly hollow
from the diligence of bees—
an apple as airy as a whiffle ball—
and buzzing, sated bees,
brawling, cider-drunk, cross-eyed,
ready to defend all trespass,
most assuredly mine;

♦♦♦

so when I cocked my arm to throw,
one, peering into my ear,
saw an apple canal and launched itself.

O what's the use?
I'm still wondering what's the lesson,
the beauty or the sting of it—
as if anything might come
of anything not promising both.
I'm wondering as if wondering weren't the answer,
the gradual dispatch of the world we trust,
the song of elision even angels can't sing,
a throaty cry, our cry.